Welfare Reform in California

State and County Implementation of CalWORKs in the First Year

EXECUTIVE SUMMARY

Gail L. Zellman
Jacob Alex Klerman
Elaine Reardon
Paul Steinberg

Prepared for the California Department of Social Services

LABOR AND POPULATION

PREFACE

In response to national welfare reform legislation—the Personal Responsibility and Work Opportunity Reconciliation Act (PRWORA), which was signed in August 1996—California passed legislation on August 11, 1997, that replaced the existing Aid to Families with Dependent Children (AFDC) and Greater Avenues to Independence (GAIN) programs with the California Work Opportunity and Responsibility to Kids (CalWORKs) program. Following an open and competitive bidding process, the California Department of Social Services (CDSS), which administers CalWORKs, awarded a contract to RAND to conduct a statewide evaluation of the CalWORKs program.

This RAND report presents an executive summary of the results from the early stages of the process study component of the evaluation. It focuses on describing the four themes that have emerged from the first process analysis.

This document draws primarily on the results of the main process analysis, which are documented in MR-1051-CDSS, *Welfare Reform in California: State and County Implementation of CalWORKs in the First Year*, 1999. The document also draws on two reports on the results of the All-County Implementation Survey (ACIS):

- MR-1052-CDSS, *Welfare Reform in California: Results of the 1998 All-County Implementation Survey*, 1999.

- MR-1052/1-CDSS, *Welfare Reform in California: Results of the 1998 All-County Implementation Survey*, Appendix, 1999.

For more information about the evaluation, see **http://www.rand.org/ CalWORKs** or contact:

Jacob Alex Klerman	Aris St. James
RAND	CDSS
1700 Main Street	744 P Street, MS 12-56
P.O. Box 2138	Sacramento, CA 95814
Santa Monica, CA 90407-2138	
(310) 393-0411 x6289	(916) 657-1959
klerman@rand.org	astjames@dss.ca.gov

CONTENTS

FIGURES

TABLES

ACKNOWLEDGMENTS

This report has been prepared under extreme time pressure. Neither the underlying analysis nor the final document could have appeared without the yeoman efforts of a large number of people.

First and foremost, we wish to thank the state and county officials who gave generously and enthusiastically of their time to help us understand CalWORKs and the changes it has engendered. Our promises of confidentiality prevent us from naming them, but they know who they are, and we appreciate their help.

Second, in organizing our field work, we have been helped by Aris St. James at the state level and the County Coordinators in each of the six focus counties: Rick Edwards, Alameda County; Denise Dotson, Butte County; Marlene Pascua, Fresno County; Althea Shirley, Los Angeles County; Kathie Stark, Sacramento County; and Ed LaBrado, San Diego County. Similarly, the senior staff in CDSS and its Research and Evaluation Branch—Bruce Wagstaff, Werner Schink, Lois VanBeers, Leslie Raderman, Paul Smilanick, and Tom Burke—have supported our efforts in ways both direct and indirect and too numerous to mention.

Within RAND, we have benefited from the formal review of Jim Dertouzos and Brent Keltner. As important have been the informal comments of many of our colleagues: Tammi Chun, Joe Hotz, Jill Humphries, Nicole Humphrey, Guido Imbens, Lynn Karoly, Elaine Reardon, Bob Reveille, Elizabeth Roth, Cathy Stasz, and Debra Strong.

Finally, a document such as this emerges because of the dedicated behind-the-scenes efforts of secretaries and publications staff members. They get the document late and are expected to make up the time in their activities. They have handled the time pressures with grace and charity. Secretaries working on this document and the project include Cherie Fields, Patrice Lester, Natasha Kostan, and Donna White. We are also grateful to the staff of RAND's Publications Department who worked on this document under an impossibly tight schedule during the December holidays. They include Betty Amo, Phyllis Gilmore, Paul Murphy, Miriam Polon, Jane Ryan, and Dan Sheehan.

ABBREVIATIONS

ACIS	RAND All-County Implementation Survey
ACL	All-County Letter
AFDC	Aid to Families with Dependent Children
CalWORKs	California Work Opportunity and Responsibility to Kids
CDSS	California Department of Social Services
EITC	Earned Income Tax Credit
GAIN	Greater Avenues to Independence
JOBS	Job Opportunities and Basic Skills (training program)
MOE	Maintenance of effort
PRWORA	Personal Responsibility and Work Opportunity Reconciliation Act
TANF	Temporary Assistance to Needy Families
Work Pays	California's Assistance Payments and Work Pays Demonstration Project

1. INTRODUCTION

Background

The Personal Responsibility and Work Opportunity Reconciliation Act of 1996 (PRWORA) fundamentally changed the American welfare system, replacing the Aid to Families with Dependent Children (AFDC) program with the Temporary Assistance to Needy Families (TANF) program. PRWORA also deliberately and decisively shifted the authority to shape welfare programs from the federal government to the individual states. California's response to PRWORA was the California Work Opportunity and Responsibility to Kids (CalWORKs) program—a "work first" program that provides support services to help recipients move from welfare to work and toward self-sufficiency. To encourage prompt transitions to work and self-sufficiency and as required by PRWORA, CalWORKs also imposes lifetime time limits. Finally, CalWORKs devolves much of the responsibility and authority for implementation to California's 58 counties, increasing counties' flexibility and financial accountability in designing their welfare programs.

PRWORA fundamentally changed America's welfare system.

CalWORKs devolves responsibility to the counties.

The California Department of Social Services (CDSS)—the state agency responsible for welfare—contracted with RAND for an independent evaluation of CalWORKs to assess both the process and its impact at both the state and county levels.

Objective

This report presents an executive summary of the results of RAND's initial process analysis, which focused on CalWORKs implementation through early December 1998. That analysis relied on three sources of information:

1. a review of pertinent documents and secondary literature concerning CalWORKs

2. the fielding (and analysis) of the RAND All-County Implementation Survey (ACIS)—a mail survey developed jointly by RAND, CDSS, and other state agencies that collected some information on the implementation of CalWORKs in each of the 58 counties

3. a series of 77 semistructured interviews with welfare agency staff at the state level and in in six preselected focus counties: Alameda, Butte, Fresno, Los Angeles, Sacramento, and San Diego.

In conducting the process analysis, RAND staff examined the historical background and context for both the federal and California welfare reform legislation and analyzed the planning process at the state and focus-county levels, the implementation status in the counties of the welfare-to-work program, and the effects CalWORKs has had to date on state and county welfare agencies.

Emerging themes provide baselines for future analysis.

Four themes emerged from this analysis—themes that provide a baseline and point to areas for investigation in the coming year. In the next four chapters, we develop these four themes. Chapter 2 examines the first theme: that welfare organizations have changed in response to the expanded mission of CalWORKs, despite the effects of limited time available for planning. Chapter 3 discusses the second theme: that implementation is under way but that recipient compliance is low. Chapter 4 presents the third theme: that the counties currently have sufficient funds but that this may change. Chapter 5 looks at the fourth theme: that achieving the kind of earnings needed to reach self-sufficiency before time limits poses a challenge. Finally, in Chapter 6, we discuss the implications these four themes have for follow-on analyses in the second-year process analysis and in the first-year impact analysis.

2. ORGANIZATIONS HAVE CHANGED IN RESPONSE TO THE EXPANDED MISSION OF CalWORKs, DESPITE LIMITED TIME FOR PLANNING

CalWORKs substantially expanded the mission of county welfare agencies. The counties needed to plan carefully and to lay the necessary groundwork for this expansion. California, however, passed its legislation later than most other states, which limited the time available for planning and rushed initial implementation. In particular, the state and the counties have been forced to put new organizational structures and management innovations in place simultaneously with new program elements.

In this chapter, we examine how the counties are responding to the need for reorganization within this limited-time planning environment.

Implementing CalWORKs Entails a Profound Expansion of the Organizational Mission

Implementing CalWORKs entails a profound change in the mission of the counties' welfare agencies. Under CalWORKs, the counties still have the mission of verifying eligibility, but now they also need to verify school attendance, immunization, and living arrangements for minors. Most critically, the counties now must strive to move almost all their caseload toward work and self-sufficiency. This entails arranging a broader range of services for recipients (job search, training, transportation, mental health, substance abuse, domestic violence), often requiring intensive case management. This expanded mission also requires performing assessments and appraisals to match services to the needs of individual recipients and implementing a sanctioning process to deal with recipient noncompliance. Finally, the counties' expanded mission creates a new "client" group to deal with: employers. To succeed, county welfare agencies need to develop positive working relationships with employers—so that they will accept job placements, work through job-placement issues, and come back to the welfare agency for new hires as initial placements move on to new jobs or up to better jobs in the same firm.

Counties must move almost all their caseloads toward work and self-sufficiency.

Late Legislation Limited the Time Available for County-Level Planning

Implementing such fundamental changes in mission is a major challenge, requiring planning and many midcourse corrections. The counties' time for planning was, however, limited by the late passage of the CalWORKs legislation. Figure 2.1 shows the key dates. California was among

California was one of the last states to reform its welfare program after PRWORA.

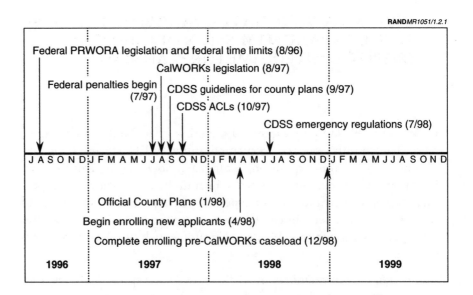

Figure 2.1—Late Legislation Limited County-Level Planning

the last states to pass legislation designed to reform its welfare system. In fact, federal PRWORA/TANF bonuses, penalties, and required maintenance of effort (MOE) levels would be computed based on participation rates from July 1997—before the CalWORKs legislation was finalized on August 11, 1997. As a result, the federal five-year clock for each welfare recipient began in November 1996, but California's five-year clock for each welfare recipient did not begin until January 1998. The state will have to pay the cost difference. In addition, the state may bear some federal penalties for having failed to meet the participation requirements before CalWORKs programs were able to move recipients into work or work activities.

The late start also limited the counties' planning period. CDSS moved quickly after the passage of the legislation to issue guidelines for official county CalWORKs plans. These guidelines, issued in an All-County Letter (ACL) in September 1997, required the counties to submit their plans to the state by January 1, 1998. Consistent with the limited time frame that emerged from the late legislation and with the legislative intent to devolve decisionmaking to the counties, CDSS informally advised the counties to prepare only minimal plans. Oversight was intentionally limited: The state did not "approve" plans; it merely "certified" that the plans addressed each of the items the legislation required and that the plans did not contradict any provision of the federal or state legislation. In-depth county-level planning was often deferred until after the official CalWORKs plan was submitted to the state.

CDSS oversight of county plans was intentionally limited.

As a Result, Counties Have Been Forced to Implement with Only Limited Planning

The timing of the passage of the CalWORKs legislation forced the counties to begin implementing their CalWORKs programs with little time for reviewing best practices, creating manuals, training staff, or pilot-testing programs. In addition, the management structures, quality-assurance systems, exception-handling policies, and data-collection systems—all of which would ideally have been in place before programs were rolled out—were often not fully developed.

Many counties did not wait for the final legislation before beginning their planning processes. These counties had been following the progress of the legislation. Even before passage of the final legislation in August 1997, many counties had done some early planning. However, some of these counties had to revise their plans to conform with the final legislation.

Some counties did early planning but had to revise plans.

Counties Are Using Different Strategies to Deal with Key Implementation Requirements

Despite the limited planning period, counties are moving forward with programs to address the key implementation requirements: (1) running eligibility and welfare-to-work activities, (2) coordinating operations with other agencies and service providers, (3) apportioning new agency responsibility to the staff, and (4) increasing the use of outsourcing. Table 2.1 shows that the focus counties have used a range of strategies to deal with these requirements.

Running Eligibility and Welfare-to-Work Activities

One of the more difficult issues counties had to face in attempting to meld welfare and work services was what to do with the old Greater Avenues to Independence (GAIN) program. Since GAIN, like the CalWORKs program, stressed training, education, and ultimate self-sufficiency for low-income clients, blending welfare and GAIN should have been straightforward. However, the two activities had very different histories and cultures and often had little experience with cooperation or communication.

Although similarly focused, GAIN and CalWORKs programs are quite different.

GAIN clients had often enrolled in activities that lasted for years at a time. Because of funding limits, GAIN often served a quarter or less of the welfare caseload and then often the more work-ready; under CalWORKs, nearly all recipients are expected to be served.

Moreover, GAIN designers had convinced relevant officials that a key component of a successful JOBS training program was to look like a business, not like a welfare office. Consequently, the appearance of GAIN offices was several notches above that of the main welfare offices.

Table 2.1

COUNTY STRATEGIES TO DEAL WITH KEY
IMPLEMENTATION REQUIREMENTS

Key Implementation Requirements	Strategies in Focus Counties
Running eligibility and welfare-to-work activities	• Range from keeping separate to merging the two welfare operations
Coordinating operations with other agencies and service providers	• Range from relying on memorandums of understanding, to colocating in "One-Stops," to issuing requests for proposals and contracts
Apportioning new agency responsibility to staff	• Range from launching reclassification studies to retraining current eligibility workers
Increasing the use of outsourcing	• Establishing formal contracts and informal coordination with community-based organizations, for-profits, and other county agencies

Merging GAIN and CalWORKs activities is a major challenge.

These realities meant that colocating GAIN and welfare staff, let alone seamlessly blending them, would be a major challenge. Ultimately, counties made very different decisions about how to deal with GAIN, with some deciding to keep GAIN separate, others deciding to merge GAIN and other welfare department activities, and still others merging GAIN and welfare activities with other departmental agencies or neighborhood centers.

Coordinating Operations with Other Agencies and Service Providers

Providing CalWORKs services requires coordinating with other agencies.

Beyond the need to deal with GAIN, welfare agencies also had to restructure to coordinate with other county agencies and community-based organizations, because welfare reform under CalWORKs provides an array of services and, thus, requires collaboration among many agencies. This collaboration had the potential to reduce duplication of effort, increase effective resources, and present to clients a seamless service-delivery system focused on shared goals.

The focus counties responded to these new demands by developing a variety of coordinating mechanisms to link agencies. Some counties merged their welfare and employment functions into multifunctional organizations ("One-Stop" shops), while others relied on memorandums of understanding to facilitate administrative integration, management, and planning.

The counties also varied in their strategies about how to coordinate activities across divisions within their own welfare departments. As noted above, in some counties, the eligibility and employment divisions remained autonomous but were housed together in a new CalWORKs bureau; in other counties, the two divisions were merged into one CalWORKs division within the welfare department. Operations that carried out duplicate functions, such as budgeting, personnel, and contracts, were also consolidated, which, according to one state-level interviewee, was a key goal of the interagency cooperation that the legislation required. Counties also used a variety of strategies to coordinate their activities with other county agencies.

The counties are also using a variety of service-delivery arrangements to provide CalWORKs services. Some counties have kept all case management, employment preparation, and placement activities in house. Others have, as much as possible, contracted these activities out to for-profit and nonprofit providers.

Counties are using different service-delivery mechanisms.

Apportioning New Agency Responsibility to Staff

Within each county's welfare organization, a major change CalWORKs imposed was the new demands it placed on eligibility workers. Before CalWORKs, eligibility workers had come to have a rather rigid gatekeeper function: Their mission was to authorize only the payments to which a family was entitled. The job focused on making sure the grant was correct. While employment and other programs might be discussed, "successful" eligibility workers were known for their low error rates: not allowing payments to which a family was not entitled. Not surprisingly, as this job took on the appearance and reality of a clerkship over time, more-qualified staff moved up or out. New eligibility workers tended to have fewer credentials in social work.

CalWORKs imposes new demands on eligibility workers.

Under CalWORKs, this eligibility worker position clearly had to change. At the same time, it had to stay the same. In addition to determining eligibility as they had always done, eligibility workers under CalWORKs would also sign up recipients for job club; educate them about CalWORKs; suggest approaches to finding work; and, in some instances, do preliminary screening for behavioral health services, including mental health, substance abuse, and domestic violence treatment. This was a "vastly different" job, according to a high-level CDSS staffer.

Several of the focus counties decided to launch reclassification studies to help determine the proper skill level and pay grade for the "new" eligibility worker, convinced that the new level would be higher than the current one. In doing these studies, these counties had the scrutiny of the unions, which indicated early on that they would be watching closely and would be weighing in as necessary as the counties planned for and implemented CalWORKs. In at least one county, union representatives sat down with welfare agency staff for the first time to talk about policy and program issues. In one of the focus counties, the union organized several rolling strikes to express concerns about the changing role of eligibility workers and opposition to the outsourcing of job club.

Reclassification studies are being launched in some counties.

Other counties decided to ask for volunteers among current eligibility workers and to train these more-motivated people to do the new job. Those who did not volunteer would continue to perform pre-CalWORKs

Some counties are training new eligibility workers.

eligibility functions and form the basis for calculating the county's error rate.

Increasing the Use of Outsourcing

Many concerns drive the use of outsourcing.

The outsourcing arrangements that were developed as part of CalWORKs implementation plans were motivated by a range of concerns, including the stability of the CalWORKs funding stream and the lack of capacity in the welfare department. As one state-level observer described it, the need to "marry off partners at the county level who had never met" has resulted in enormous change: These changes include formal contracts and informal coordination with the community-based service providers, for-profits, and other county agencies that would actually deliver some or all the services newly available to clients of the welfare department.

3. IMPLEMENTATION IS UNDER WAY, BUT RECIPIENT COMPLIANCE IS LOW

The core of the federal PRWORA and the state CalWORKs legislation is work. The legislation imposes strong work requirements; provides services to help recipients find work; and expects that, through work, individuals will achieve self-sufficiency within only a few years. In particular, the CalWORKs legislation, following the approach of the Riverside GAIN program and the 1995 revisions to the statewide GAIN program, specifies a sequence of activities for welfare recipients. The sequence of activities is explicitly "work first," although the legislation is written loosely enough to allow the counties considerable discretion in the design of their welfare-to-work programs.

The core of both PRWORA and CalWORKs is work.

This chapter examines the current status of county implementation efforts and focuses on the noncompliance problems that are already surfacing.

Implementation Is Under Way but Is Far from Complete

The CalWORKs legislation mandated that the counties follow a sequence of activities in implementing their welfare-to-work programs: enrollment, job club/job search, assessment, work activities (work experience, training, education), and then community-service work. The list of exemptions from these activities is deliberately short, the main one being the presence of a very young child (by default, six months; at county option, three to twelve months, and for only one child). Under CalWORKs, a much greater proportion of recipients is expected to participate than did under the old GAIN program.

Counties must follow a sequence of mandated activities.

Not surprisingly, the earlier activities—enrollment and job club/job search—are more fully implemented, while the later steps—assessment and work activities and community service—have often barely begun or are just being planned:

- **Enrollment.** As of the spring of 1998, new recipients were immediately enrolled in CalWORKs, and that transition appears to have gone smoothly. All the existing AFDC caseload was to have been enrolled in CalWORKs by January 1, 1999. Nearly all counties told us they would meet the deadline. Now that the deadline has passed, nearly all have met this goal. However, doing so often required major efforts (e.g., staff overtime, night and weekend hours).

Almost all counties met the enrollment deadline.

- **Job Club.** For nonworking recipients, the next step after enrollment is job club. In the fall of 1998, counties were massively expanding their job club programs to absorb what they expected to be much larger flows of people. Every county appears to have its job club efforts up and running.

- **Assessment and Work Activity.** After job club, the CalWORKs legislation calls for an assessment and then a work activity. Job club activities appear to be in place nominally, but the flow of people out of job club is still so small that there is little to observe or evaluate.

- **Community Service.** For those who finish work activities and still do not have a job, the CalWORKs legislation calls for community service. Community service plans are still being devised; the first mandatory assignment to community service will not occur until July 1999 at the earliest.

High Job-Placement Rates Mask a Noncompliance Problem

Job-placement rates are high . . .

Many counties are claiming great success with job club: Of those who participate in job club, job-placement rates appear to be quite high, somewhere between 60 and 85 percent. However, two caveats are crucial. First, these figures refer to "those who participate," which turns out to be a small fraction of those assigned (often a third or less). Second, the jobs that constitute "success" are often part time, at or near minimum wage, and of short duration. We will return to the implications of the second caveat in our discussion of the fourth theme.

. . . but only for those who participate.

Here, we focus on the first caveat: the noncompliance problem. Such noncompliance is not surprising or unique to CalWORKs; high no-show rates were also apparent under GAIN.

Some view noncompliance as a temporary problem of conveying new expectations.

Observers have different perspectives on this noncompliance. One perspective of noncompliance posits that CalWORKs places new expectations on welfare recipients and that, as word "hits the street" that participation really is required and that failure to cooperate will lead to sanctions, compliance will increase. Some proponents of the first perspective also argue that there are barriers that hinder participation for some would-be participants; for example, some cannot understand the notices because they do not speak English. In addition, proponents of this perspective argue that some would-be recipients have resource barriers—the need for child care or transportation—and are not aware that CalWORKs will provide such resources to enable participation. Finally, those advocating this perspective argue that some recipients have work barriers, such as substance abuse or mental health problems, that prevent them from participating or even requesting the services they would need to participate. According to this view, counties need to dedicate staff to helping recipients overcome their barriers to participation in CalWORKs activities.

Another perspective posits that noncompliance is a deliberate choice not to participate. Those holding this perspective suspect that the recipients who do not comply have significant levels of unreported ("under the table") labor earnings. In addition, they argue that the details of the CalWORKs legislation actually *encourage* noncompliance. They point, in particular, to the fact that sanctions only eliminate the adult portion of the family's grant; the larger child portion continues, along with MediCal and Food Stamps. Moreover, when the sanction is imposed, the adult's five-year clock on lifetime welfare receipt stops. Thus, for some recipients, being sanctioned can be desirable: They are not participating in the welfare-to-work activity; they still receive most of their grant; and their 60-month time-limit clock stops.

Some view noncompliance as a deliberate choice not to participate.

Although Counties Are Still Developing Sanction Programs, Many Are Concerned They Will Be Ineffective When in Place

The counties are at various stages in the process of sanctioning no-shows. Some counties are not sanctioning at all; some are just rolling out their sanction programs; and some have sanction programs in place. The overall lack of sanction programs is corroborated by ACIS data for all 58 counties. The data show that only 15 of the counties report that a vendor voucher system, which is necessary to implement the full sanction sequence, is fully operational countywide. Most (33 counties) reported that planning or design for such a system was "in progress," and 7 indicated they had not planned or designed the system.

Sanctioning programs are not fully operational in many counties.

Why are sanctioning programs not more widespread? This process is cumbersome and expensive in the face of high nonparticipation rates, since multiple attempts by employment caseworkers to contact clients considered to be uncooperative take time away from other activities. One key issue is the amount of coordination necessary to implement a sanction. Although caseworkers decide whether a sanction is required, they do not apply it; instead, they refer the case to an eligibility worker for processing.

Another issue is the effect of sanctions. First, interviewees noted that the penalty is small. California—to protect children—continues to impose only a limited (adult grant only) sanction even for continued failure to comply with work requirements. For a family of three with no other earnings, this amounts to a loss of only $118 out of the full CalWORKs grant of $611.

Sanctions are not large.

Second, the process is not swift. Part of the problem is that computer systems in some counties are not generating the right types of notices, so the process must be handled manually. Similarly, some computer systems are not properly computing the grant if a sanction is imposed, so again, the computation must be done by hand. However, even if the notices were sent more quickly, there is often a significant delay in

Sanctions are not swift.

imposing the sanctions once the notices do go out. Failure to cooperate with work requirements results in a 20-day grace period, which often pushes the grant reduction from the month after noncompliance to the following month. This long delay obscures the relationship between noncompliance and its consequences.

Sanctions are not sure.

Third, the sanction is not sure. Sanctions may be waived for "good cause." Some counties are using a sufficiently broad definition of "good cause" that simply contacting the case worker will remove the sanction. Furthermore, removal of the sanction often simply puts the recipient back into the queue for job club.

4. COUNTIES CURRENTLY HAVE SUFFICIENT FUNDS, BUT THIS MAY CHANGE

The deep recession of the early 1990s and the ensuing budget crisis for the state and counties prevented broad implementation of the last major welfare reform in California—GAIN. However, for CalWORKs, the economic conditions and program funding are quite different. As the counties roll out their CalWORKs programs, per-case funds for welfare-to-work activities and other support services are significantly higher than in the years immediately before the reform. Whether this high level of funding will continue as is, become more pronounced, or shrink is less clear.

Currently, economic conditions and program funding for CalWORKs are good.

Much of the implementation of CalWORKs involves the unfolding implications of this higher funding level. In this chapter, we examine why the funding levels are higher, reasons such funding levels may not continue, and how counties are responding to the high level of funding.

The Counties Currently Have Sufficient Funds

The higher level of funding under CalWORKs is the result of a number of factors, including the shift from separate funding streams to a single TANF block grant, the addition of other welfare-related funding streams, the decline in caseloads, and the carryover of unspent funds from previous years.

The Shift to a Single TANF Block Grant

In keeping with the federal and California determination to devolve control and responsibility for welfare reform to lower levels (to the states in PRWORA and to the counties in CalWORKs), both the federal and state legislation converted many of the previously targeted funding streams into block grants. In particular, PRWORA converted the previously separate AFDC, emergency assistance, and JOBS funding into a single TANF block grant. The magnitude of the block grant was based on nominal expenditures in the 1992 to 1996 period but was not indexed for inflation. Since then, the economy has improved; caseloads have declined; and inflation has been low. As a result, federal dollars under TANF are higher than they would have been under the prereform rules.

CalWORKs converted many previous funding streams into block grants.

In addition, to prevent major cuts in funding at lower levels of government, federal legislation imposed a MOE requirement on the states. This MOE is designed to prevent states from reallocating previous state welfare funds to other programs not related to welfare. Instead, the MOE required the states to spend 75 or 80 percent of their funding for welfare programs in the baseline period. The lower figure was to apply to states that satisfied the TANF work requirements; however, most states (including California) have not met the two-parent work requirements and have therefore been held to the higher MOE requirement.

Other Funding Streams

PRWORA and follow-on legislation provided other funding streams.

In addition to the increase in funds from the block grants, the states also received additional funding from PRWORA and follow-on legislation. Partially in reaction to President Clinton's original veto of welfare reform legislation in January 1996, the final PRWORA legislation included additional child-care funds. Furthermore, the Balanced Budget Act of 1997 included funding for a new stream of welfare-to-work dollars, administered through the Department of Labor, to provide training and supported work experience for the hardest-to-employ welfare populations. Furthermore, the welfare-to-work funds required matching state expenditures. These child-care and training funds have further raised federal dollars to the states over what would have been available (or had been available) under AFDC.

Declining Caseloads

Caseloads in California are declining.

Another factor that has been key to the increase in funding levels is the decline in welfare caseloads throughout the country. While the decline in California from its peak in January 1995 to June 1998 was 25 percent, far less than the national average of 40 percent, it is nevertheless substantial. For fixed total funding (such as the block grants plus the MOE), a smaller caseload implies more resources per case.

Carryover Funds

The above three factors relate to the level of new funding available. In addition, California's late legislation and the resulting delayed rollout of CalWORKs programs led the state to underspend PRWORA funds over the last two years. These carryover funds increase the amount available to the counties this year.

How Much Do These Factors Affect Per-Case Funding?

Per-case funding has increased by 10 percent.

Taken together, the block grants, new funding streams, and caseload declines have increased the net per-case dollars. The block grant is higher in total than it would have been under the prereform formula, and per-case funding is thus much higher. The 80-percent MOE based on a high spending year kept state expenditures per case approximately constant. The new funding streams and their required matching state expenditures further increased total funding, and thus per-case funding, even more. In net, it appears that funds per case have increased about 10 percent. In addition, the carryover funding represents another 10-percent increase in total available dollars.

Counties' Fiscal Status Could Change Dramatically

Whether the counties will continue to have high levels of funding is an open question. The answer will depend on internal and external factors.

Internal Factors

The internal factors center on the potential tightening of the funding situation from the maturing of the CalWORKs program itself. The amount of money per case that counties will need to spend may grow in the future as the programs they are implementing mature. The counties are still rolling out their programs. Through late 1998, the counties have focused on relatively inexpensive activities—enrollment and job search. They have done so partially because of the mandated sequence of activities, partially because of the conscious choice of the counties, and partially because of the behaviors of recipients. The later steps—such as training and supported work—will be more expensive to serve per case. In addition, as mentioned above, welfare recipients are eligible for child care, transportation, mental-health treatment, substance-abuse treatment, and domestic-violence counseling—services and programs that can be very expensive. Currently, referrals for such supportive services is low but is expected to grow.

Funding later work activities is more expensive . . .

. . . and demand for expensive services is likely to grow.

In addition, while caseloads have declined in California, they could decline even further. At the national level, the declines were simultaneous with a continuously robust economy and the implementation of PRWORA programs and their stronger work requirements. In California, as noted above, the legislation passed late, and implementation is not as advanced as it is nationally. Thus, as implementation progresses in California, caseloads would be expected to decline further, assuming the economy remains robust. As important, the amount of the grant would decline as recipients go to work—even if they continue to receive some cash grant. Combined with block grants and the MOE, these changes would increase funding per case.

Further declines would increase funds per case.

External Factors

Beyond these internal factors, there are also some external reasons the funding level may change. The standard threats to the financial health of welfare programs remain. In the same way that the current robust economy has driven caseloads down, a worsening economy could drive caseloads up. How far is unclear, but as of now, the counties are setting aside little of the available funds for such a contingency.

The carryover funds discussed above may be consumed. If so, in 2000–2001 and following years, total federal funding would return to the block-grant level, 10 percent below this year's level.

Finally, changes in the level of funding are also possible. If caseloads remain at their current levels or drop further, there is the possibility that politicians—whether at the federal, state, or county level—will reallocate the funds to other, nonwelfare population uses or at least to "rainy day" funds. Federal and state legislation, regulations, and MOEs limit the scope for such transfers, but some latitude appears to remain.

Funds could be reallocated away from welfare populations.

As a Result, the Responses of County Welfare Agencies Vary

Given the uncertainty over future funding, the counties are, not surprisingly, taking approaches to implementation that vary in their level of cautiousness. For example, some counties are hiring new staff, while others have resolved to put off hiring new staff. In addition, some counties are initiating new programs, while some are allocating funds to strengthen infrastructure for a "rainy day."

On the possibility that current funding conditions will continue or further improve, some counties are considering significant expansions of the mission and activities of their agencies. These expanded visions involve going beyond simply verifying the eligibility of the current caseload (as was true before CalWORKs) or even helping current recipients find jobs (as is mandated by CalWORKs); these visions also include providing intensive job-retention services and training for recent recipients, taking social-work approaches (i.e., intensive and extensive one-to-one contact between the recipient and a skilled caseworker) to current recipients, and even offering services to the working poor.

Some counties are considering expanding their mission and activities.

Presumably, if funds get tight—whether because of the maturing of the CalWORKs program, because of an economic downturn, or because of reallocation of resources—counties will reconsider the menu of services they offer. They would be expected to limit the availability of some, cut the per-case resources for others, and eliminate some entirely. Such behavior has been observed in earlier episodes of budget tightening.

5. ACHIEVING EARNINGS NEEDED TO ACHIEVE SELF-SUFFICIENCY BEFORE TIME LIMITS EXPIRE IS A CHALLENGE

PRWORA at the federal level and CalWORKs in California make two fundamental changes in welfare programs. First, recipients are expected to work or engage in specified welfare-to-work activities. Second, and arguably more important, welfare is no longer an indefinite entitlement. Lifetime receipt of cash assistance is limited to five years for adults. In California, the child portion of the grant can continue indefinitely. This time limit imparts an urgency to all welfare-to-work activities. Families need to move promptly and decisively toward work and self-sufficiency.

CalWORKs is a "work first" program.

The CalWORKs legislation clearly implies a "work first" approach. The slogan in several of the counties is "A Job; a Better Job; a Career," where a career is understood to be a job that enables self-sufficiency. Under CalWORKs, it clearly pays for recipients to work. However, moving current recipients off of cash assistance to self-sufficiency—a career—is considerably more challenging.

In this chapter, we discuss how the current structure of CalWORKs encourages recipients to work and how challenging it will be to move recipients off cash assistance and to self-sufficiency altogether.

Under CalWORKs, Work Pays

One approach to moving recipients toward self-sufficiency is to construct the benefit schedule in such a way as to make work more attractive than welfare. CalWORKs continues and extends the changes made in the state's earlier Work Pays Demonstration to encourage work. In each month, after the first $225 dollars, the CalWORKs participant has his or her grant decreased one dollar for every two dollars of earned income. In addition, the federal government has recently increased the Earned Income Tax Credit (EITC). These changes have the net effect of making cash aid slightly less valuable for those not working and more valuable for those working more than a minimal amount.

CalWORKs continues and extends earlier changes to encourage work.

What this all means for a family of three (after the 1998 increases in the cash payment) is that work pays, as summarized below in Figure 5.1. The figure shows how total household resources change as household earned income increases. The horizontal axis varies household earned income. The vertical axis varies total household resources—including earned income (the light gray area under the 45-degree line), the CalWORKs grant (the darker gray area), and other government transfers (including Food Stamps and the EITC, less payroll taxes; the hatch-marked band).

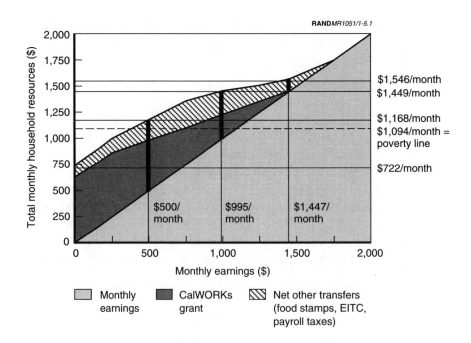

Figure 5.1—With CalWORKs Grant Structure, Work Pays

As the figure shows on the vertical axis, those not working end up with a package of CalWORKs and other transfers that amounts to total monthly household resources of less than $722 per month, well below the poverty line of $1,094 per month. However, we see that the total package implies that even minimal earnings—half time at the minimum wage ($5.75 per hour for total monthly earnings of about $500)—will lift a family of three out of poverty. At this level of earnings, as shown by the vertical line to the far left, total monthly household resources amount to $1,168, which is 7 percent above the poverty line of $1,094. The bolded part of the $500 vertical line shows that these earnings are supplemented by a significant package of benefits, with the bulk coming from the CalWORKs grant.

Under CalWORKs, working even half time at minimum wage pays.

A full-time minimum-wage job pays even better. As shown in the figure, full-time employment at the minimum wage ($5.75 per hour for total monthly earnings of about $995) yields total household resources of $1,449 (shown by the vertical line in the middle), which is 32 percent above the poverty line. At this point, the package of benefits (as shown by the bolded part of the line) relies almost equally on the CalWORKs grant and the other transfers.

Full-time work at $8.36 an hour will move a family of three off aid.

While moving recipients to this level would lift them out of poverty, they cannot receive this $1,449 package indefinitely. After 60 months, time limits would cause recipients to lose the adult portion of the CalWORKs grant. What kind of a job does a family of three require to be ineligible for any cash grant? The figure shows us that a family of three will need a full-time job paying $8.36 an hour, $1,447 per month (yielding total household resources of $1,546, as shown by the far right vertical line), to be ineligible for cash assistance. In this case, as shown by the bolded part of the line, the augmentation to earnings comes entirely from the other transfers.

Moving Recipients to Self-Sufficiency Is Challenging

While there is a potential pathway to self-sufficiency through work, getting current recipients jobs with sufficient hours and with high-enough wages, before the time limits expire, will prove challenging.

For most current recipients who are willing to work, California's robust economy might be able to create a job. However, one of the concerns arising from our conversations with county officials is the issue of job quality and wage growth: What kinds of jobs will recipients get and keep? There is concern that aid recipients will find work in part-time, short-term, and dead-end jobs that offer little hope of self-sufficiency. The skills of many recipients may not be deemed worthy of compensation several dollars above the minimum wage. In addition, some individuals will have multiple barriers to employment.

The issue of job quality and wage growth is critical.

Riverside County's GAIN program has been pointed to as a successful JOBS training program. With strong local political support, Riverside's GAIN program established a work-first orientation, and it made a difference. Analysis using randomized assignment found that, compared to the conventional program over the first three years, Riverside's Work First raised employment rates (35 percent versus 24 percent), increased earnings (by 50 percent), and lowered welfare payments (by $1,400 over two years).

The example of Riverside GAIN shows the challenge CalWORKs faces.

However, even for this successful program, most of the experimental group were not even working full time five years later, most were receiving welfare, and very few were making the equivalent of $8.36 an hour at a full-time, full-year job. Clearly, the state and the counties have a great deal of work ahead to design and implement programs that move all but 20 percent of recipients to self-sufficiency.

Counties Need to Work to Meet the Challenge

At this point, it is too early to know how well counties will meet the challenge of moving recipients to self-sufficiency. It is possible the economy will remain strong and will produce jobs and that the average CalWORKs program—given what has been learned about welfare-to-work programs, given higher funding levels, and given CalWORKs' rich menu of support services—will be much more effective than the Riverside GAIN program. And perhaps the threat of time limits—not present in the GAIN program—will serve as an additional motivator.

It seems almost certain that the results will be heterogeneous. Some recipients will move quickly and steadily toward self-sufficiency; some

Outcomes are likely to be heterogeneous.

will move into the work force and full-time jobs, but at wages not much above the minimum wage; some will work only part time or for part of the year; and some will not work at all. Some recipients may hit the time limits; some may voluntarily remove themselves from the welfare rolls before hitting time limits, to maintain their eligibility in the event of future reversals; and some may accept sanctions to stop their time-limit clocks while continuing to receive cash assistance for their children. The distribution of the caseload into these groups will become apparent over the next few years, and the impact analysis should provide preliminary indications.

CalWORKs has a number of pluses to help it meet the challenge.

While meeting the challenge will be difficult, CalWORKs does have a number of pluses working in its favor. For one thing, unlike GAIN and other past welfare reform efforts, CalWORKs has the funding to implement a wide range of support services to enable welfare recipients to overcome barriers to work. In addition, the larger caseload declines in states with more mature TANF programs are encouraging. Finally, our fieldwork revealed a reservoir of enthusiasm from the counties, with a strong determination among staff to help people change.

6. IMPLICATIONS FOR FOLLOW-ON ACTIVITIES

The results reported in this executive summary are based on only three months of fieldwork. While it is too early in the implementation of CalWORKs and in our evaluation of it to reach definitive conclusions, we have identified the four emerging themes discussed above. These themes, in turn, can be used as a guide for the continuing fieldwork and quantitative analysis to be conducted over the remaining two and a half years of the evaluation. More specifically, each of the four themes suggests specific follow-on analyses, which are summarized in Table 6.1. Each set of follow-on analyses is discussed in more detail below.

The emerging themes suggest follow-on analyses.

Theme 1: Organizational Change

Because we were only able to spend a few days in each of the six focus counties and have talked almost exclusively to senior staff in state and county welfare agencies, we have an incomplete understanding of the programs the counties have implemented and the institutional mechanisms they are using to do so. Further fieldwork will allow us to track county planning and interagency interactions more fully. Our semistructured interviews to date have focused on senior staff in the welfare agencies. Policy, however, is implemented and often altered by lower-level employees—office directors, supervisors, and caseworkers. Over the next year, our investigation will extend down to welfare offices, caseworkers, and recipients. In addition, since the CalWORKs legislation

Further fieldwork will help to better track state, county, and interagency interactions.

Table 6.1

EMERGING THEMES AND THEIR IMPLICATIONS FOR
FOLLOW-ON ANALYSES

Emerging Theme	Follow-On Analyses
1. Organizations are responding to the expanded mission of CalWORKs, despite limited time for planning	• Track planning and interagency interactions • Describe organizational and institutional changes; assess impacts on line staff and recipients
2. Implementation is under way, but recipient compliance is low	• Characterize the normal program flow • Investigate noncompliance and sanctions
3. Counties currently have sufficient funds, but this may change	• Build a better flow of funds model • Model costs per activity • Monitor how counties spend funds
4. Achieving earnings needed for self-sufficiency before time limits expire is a challenge	• In impact analysis, track employment and earnings

envisions providing a wide range of services to welfare recipients, spanning not only multiple state and county agencies but also community-based organizations and for-profit enterprises, our investigation will also expand to allied agencies at the state and county levels, to nonprofit organizations, and to for-profit firms. Through these efforts, we hope to gain a better understanding of what CalWORKs programs are and how they differ across the counties.

Theme 2: Implementation and Noncompliance

Analyzing administrative data systems will allow quantification of the status of implementation.

Our understanding of the status of counties' implementation efforts has so far been based on the reports of senior county welfare department staff. We are currently processing the state and county administrative data systems and the official county reports to the state. When processing is complete, we will be able to augment the impressions of county welfare officials with tabulations from the official administrative data systems. These tabulations will tell us the number of recipients in each activity, how the individual recipients flow through the welfare system, and how the system is changing over time. Just as important, these measures will be more consistent across time and across counties.

Low recipient-compliance levels suggest several follow-on research activities. The fall fieldwork made clear that notification procedures, compliance, and sanctions would be key implementation issues. Follow-on analyses will more carefully explore notification and sanctioning procedures and how they evolve over time. Furthermore, the administrative data systems should allow numerical estimates of the prevalence of noncompliance and of sanctions.

Theme 3: Sufficiency of Funding

Collecting more-detailed financial information will allow a better understanding of budgetary conditions.

Our characterization of county funding levels was based on conversations with senior county officials and simple tabulations from published budget summaries. We are now collecting detailed financial information for the state and for the counties. With that information, we will be able to construct better estimates of the available funding and how it is being used. To project future expenses, we will explore costs per activity and the flows of individuals between activities. Finally, we will carefully monitor potential changes in the external environment, such as funding levels and changes in labor market conditions.

Theme 4: Transition to Self-Sufficiency

As was true with the others, this theme suggests clear directions for future analysis—particularly, the impact analysis. While one focus of the impact analysis needs to be on evaluating the *net* effect of CalWORKs relative to some other policy (e.g., AFDC, TANF in other states,

CalWORKs across counties), this theme suggests that there are *absolute* standards—self-sufficiency, receipt of any cash grant, resources greater than the poverty level—that are arguably as interesting. The effect of time limits will depend crucially on the success of CalWORKs recipients in moving into the work force and toward self-sufficiency. Thus, the impact analysis will track the extent to which recipients are finding any job and finding a full-time job. Beyond employment, the impact analysis needs to track wages and, more important, earnings (by month, by quarter, by year). After the first job, success of the CalWORKs program will require that recipients follow a career ladder from any job, to a better job (or at least the same job with higher wages), to a career (job). Simultaneously, the impact analysis needs to track the accumulation of months toward time limits—tracking temporary setbacks (returns to welfare and job loss)—and, more broadly, household resources, health insurance coverage, poverty, and child living arrangements.

Tracking how recipients move into the labor force and toward self-sufficiency will be part of the impact analysis.

Future reports will document the results of these follow-on analyses, the evolution of the CalWORKs program, and its effects on program participants.